WHEN

The Critical

LOVE

Importance

IS NOT

of Knowledgeable

ENOUGH

Parenting

By Miriam Kove

WHEN LOVE IS NOT ENOUGH:

The Critical Importance Of Knowledgeable Parenting

DEDICATION

To my wonderful grandchildren, Noble and Sera,
who teach me every day the nature and obligations of love.

WHEN LOVE IS NOT ENOUGH:
The Critical Importance Of Knowledgeable Parenting

Most parents love their children deeply and want the very best for them.
Yet, in the United States, suicide is the third leading cause of death among
teenagers aged 15-24. Mental health disorders such as depression and substance
abuse are heavily linked to suicide and mental health disorders are often caused
by traumas and difficult childhoods. In these United States, 877,802 individuals
aged 20 years or younger were treated in ER drug related complications and
approximately 438,000 of these teenagers had already abused drugs over long
periods of time. Substance abuse disorders are related to suicide and related to
traumatic and difficult childhoods. Why do we refuse to see the connections?

John lived on a farm. He rose at 4:30 A.M. when he was four and did a series of
chores dictated by his father. If the chores were not done perfectly, his father would
take him outside into the ten-degree harsh snow, strip his pants down and beat him.
When he cried because the pain and humiliation were horrific, his father beat him
more. Cynthia was eight when her stepfather insisted that she watch him and her
mother have sex so that she would know "what it was all about."
Wyatt was told by his "dear" Mother that, every time he misbehaved, "the bad
boy agency" was coming to take him. He had no explanation for what the bad boy
agency might be but it felt ominous and dark, and to be taken away from home
was unthinkable, so Wyatt grew up terrified of everything and organizing himself as
"bad," and, subsequently, killing himself with drugs. Terrence, at six, was ordered to
chaperone his sister on dates and, for the next ten years, he was forced to abandon
his own interests and friends to adhere to his sister's schedule.

The confusion in him about what he saw and heard and couldn't understand, skewed his view of himself and the world forever.

Tatiana was not permitted to have a feeling or an idea. If she cried or sneezed or said that she was hungry, her mother would automatically hit her on the head with a wooden spoon that she always carried with her. Tatiana learned to be "dead" and mute. Ivan was allowed nothing in his family- no toys, no friends, no advanced schooling- only food. Food was plentiful and permissible. Today, Ivan is 150 pounds overweight and has no life at all. He is giving himself only what his parents allowed him -- food. Esther's mother was a busy lawyer, saving the world. Esther was left under the total care of a nanny who systematically molested her on a regular basis and terrified her into silence.

These scenarios exist in many, many homes and are much more prevalent than we want to believe. Yet, even where the home is safer and parents more benign, neglect and abuse are seen everywhere. Mary loves her three-year-old son and hugs and kisses him frequently. Yet, she denied him access to the parental bedroom, a bedroom where the new sister is allowed to visit and sleep. She doesn't understand, that feeling abandoned already and replaced by his sibling, her son will feel more abandoned and displaced and unimportant by this exclusion.

Tom is a very big executive and, when he is with his children at the park or at dinner, he is constantly on his phone, calling and texting, busy and distraced while his children desperately vie for his attention to no avail. Tom does not understand how negatively this will impact his children's self-esteem. Cynthia is very angry with her son. He's three and not toilet trained. Her daughter was toilet trained in two days. Cynthia fails to understand that children are different and have different readiness. And so it goes, well meaning parents engaging in behaviors that will be hurtful and destructive to their innocent children and doing it out of ignorance --

Whatever career one chooses, there is an education to be had, tests to be passed, internships to be navigated, licenses to be acquired, endless rites, rituals and formalities to be observed before one can hang out a shingle. Yet, parenting, the most critical career of all, a career that will hugely impact the life of not only one child but all the people he interacts with, that determines the quality of the citizens of our society requires nothing but the desire to have a child and a biological capability so we can come to the task of raising a child unknowing and unthinking.

We are parenting in three different styles. The most common style is that we do what is comfortable and easy and pleasurable to ourselves. While we're choosing this, we are ignoring the needs of the child and the consequences of our behavior.

Sarah is a harried Mom. She's a nurse in the emergency room of a major hospital, responsible to endless people and working under critical and difficult circumstances. When she comes home to her eleven month old baby, she's exhausted. Her solution is to send the baby to grandmother's every weekend for the whole weekend. She doesn't understand why the baby screams and cries before she goes and comes home dejected and depressed. She doesn't understand that for an eleven month old baby the only safety in the universe is experienced with the Mother. For a helpless, powerless eleven month old baby who can't do anything for herself, the Mother is experienced as the source of comfort and supplies and life itself and that without the "Powerful Other," there is only the abyss.

9.

She doesn't understand that at eleven months, children experience a particular stage of "stranger anxiety" where others are experienced as foreign and dangerous. She doesn't understand that she's probably gestating in her baby an abandonment depression syndrome which will be very detrimental to her beloved child.

Ann and Sam lead hectic lives. They're frazzled and tired. When their two-year-old wakes in the middle of the night, it's so much easier to let him sleep in their bed rather than comfort him in his. This will continue for eight years when their son will refuse to have overnights with friends and family and therapeutic intervention will be necessary.

Scarlett's son, Scott, cannot enter a supermarket without insisting that he buy five sugar cereals. When Scarlett attempts to ration the cereal or change the agenda, Scott throws a full temper tantrum in the middle of the store. Scarlett allows him to do exactly as he pleases so she can maintain peace and an unembarrassed comfort zone for herself.

And so it goes.

The second style of parenting is to repeat the parenting that one has experienced.

Arnold and Betty brought their son into treatment because he was severely depressed and failing in school. In exploration, one of the issues that emerged is that in his own growing up, Arnold's parents had disciplined him with the "hand from the floor" threat. They warned him that, if he were "bad," the floor would open, a giant hand would emerge and it would drag him under. Although this never happened, he believed them implicitly and grew up meek and terrified, though functioning. He employed this same method with his son who, less strong emotionally, became too terrified to function.

Didi's mother was a failed actress absorbed with her appearance. Didi was her beauty creation. Appearance was the only factor that was emphasized. Endless hours were spent in discussion about hair and eyebrows and clothes. Skin was minutely examined for flaws. Trends in fashion were slavishly explored and followed. At four, Didi became a beauty pageant contestant and remained one until she was twenty and married. At three years old, her daughter, Minerva, is a beauty pageant contestant as well, even though Minerva throws up before every event, desperately asks her Mother not to go, hides in the closet to escape. There is no escape.

Sandy and Ed both came from homes where discipline was equated with hitting. Whenever there was an infraction, wherever they happened to be, the Father would take off his belt and let them have it. No matter how painful and humiliating these experiences were, they repeated them with their son. When they were urged by the school counselor to seek help for their son, they came to treatment. They were shocked and astonished to learn that there existed other forms of discipline besides beatings.

The third style of parenting is to veer in the exact opposite direction of one's experience. Ruth was a Holocaust child. She spent her first three years in a concentration camp, without food, without medicine, without clothes, without toys, without any kind of safety. Pained and deprived and deeply sad, she vowed that her children would have a blissful childhood of plenty.

Smart and disciplined, she created a golden time for her children. What she failed to realize is that over protection and over coddling provide their own negative outcomes. Her children came into a grownup world that didn't give them what they wanted, did not perceive them as "special," could be callous and abusive and humiliating and abandoning. They were shocked and ignorant and had great difficulty finding their way.

As an adolescent, Cassandra was hounded by her Mother. She would be stopped at the door before exiting. Her dress and makeup were minutely inspected. Every "infraction" was criticized and ordered to change. When she went out with her friends, she was expected to give minute details of her plans and to call home every hour to report that she was okay. When her Mother didn't like a friend, she was ordered to drop that friend immediately, without discussion.
She was never permitted overnights at all under any circumstances.
Cassandra felt trapped, caged and helpless.

When her own children became teenagers, she remembered and gave them complete freedom: no rules, no limits, no discussions or education on sex, drugs, alcohol...They were free to find their own way. When her daughter was brought home by the police, drunk and injured, having totaled her car and barely escaped with her life, Cassandra woke up.

Betsy had a childhood of endless activity. Every minute was scheduled and organized. There was tutoring and piano lessons and the chess club and the hockey team and the debating team and swimming lessons... Betsy remembers her childhood as racing from one activity to another, from one place to another,

12.

frazzled and overwhelmed, terrified that she would miss something or be late for something. There was no time to just "be," to relax, to dream, to rest, to fantasize. Betsy remembered all this with sadness and dismay. Her Robin's life would not be like that. Her Robin's life would be endless time spent in freedom so no activities or hobbies were offered; no play dates were discussed; no activities were arranged. There was school and endless empty time. One day, when Robin was 9, Betsy found her sitting on the floor in the kitchen, crying and telling the cat how bored she was.

I'm advocating a fourth style of parenting. The hallmark of this style of parenting is <u>consciousness, knowledge and competence.</u>
Children are not little adults. They are different beings at different ages and stages.
As children grow, they pass through a variety of different ages and stages.
Each stage is marked by different needs, has different tasks to be accomplished by the child and has different physical, psychological and social milestones to be reached by the child.

For example: At three years old, a child is usually in a state of equilibrium. Physically, he is sure on his feet. He walks well and he runs easily, swings his arms with ease. Socially he now likes other children and enjoys them. But, most of all, he enjoys his Mother. He loves to be with her, share activities with her, help her with the housework, have her read to him, etc. Emotionally, the typical three-year-old is a happy person, calm, collected, friendly and cooperative. He loves to please. He also loves words, to learn them, to play with them, and to respond to them. Discipline at this age and stage can be distraction with words e.g. offering a <u>surprise</u> can quickly save a situation that is beginning to deteriorate.

At three and a half, a new person emerges. Three and a half refuses to obey. He uses his will to oppose his Mother. Even the simplest event, dressing, bedtime can erupt in rebellion. The three and a half year old child is anxious, insecure and confused. Even physically, he has changed. He stumbles, he shuffles, he stutters, he may suck his thumb, rub his genitals, pick his nose.

To make him feel more sure of himself - the three and a half year old tries to control his environment by ordering and commanding people - "don't talk," "don't look" - not letting Father talk on the phone or Mother read her newspaper.
He wants all the attention, is not interested in cooperation and can make life very difficult for his parents.

For a parent who does not understand ages and stages, this sudden stage would be a confusion and a horror. How did their charming, obliging three-year-old turn into this monster? Parents might respond with shock, dismay, great anxiety. They might feel that they had done something horribly wrong. They might feel guilty and ashamed or they might become very angry and engage in punitive measures to make the child "behave" - screaming, hitting, excessive times out, criticizing, abandoning. This could be a destructive time for both parents and children.

The knowledgeable parent, however, the one who understands ages and stages, is prepared. He or she understands that this behavior is normal, to be expected, that it will pass. The knowledgeable parent can devise or learn strategies that work in this period of disequilibrium. The knowledgeable parent understands that the child is not being malicious or manipulative and has no control over what is

14.

happening to him physically and emotionally, that he may be more uncomfortable and unhappy than they are. The knowledgeable parent can help.

Since the most difficult times with a three-and-a-half-year-old are experienced in interactions between a child and his Mother, this would be a good time to provide a nursery school or a baby sitter. The child will behave better with a substitute caregiver and the Mother can have some peace to husband her strength. However, in the time the Mother is with the child, she can give him time to play with her - children at this age love to play. She can give him physical and verbal affection to boost his self-esteem. Another strategy is to "learn" your child well and to recognize his triggers. If he becomes "undone" in the supermarket or a toy store, keep him away from those situations. If some routine is especially difficult, find some creative way to diffuse the situation. Gloria had great trouble with dressing. She refused her Mother's suggestions and confused herself by changing her mind every few minutes. Her Mother created a "dressing genie" who would whisper her suggestions in Gloria's ear. Gloria was enchanted and what was difficult became easy. Tom would refuse to get up in the morning and come to breakfast. His father devised a "surprise" strategy. Every morning at the breakfast table, there would be something new - a penny, a sticker, a little book...

Tom was excited and delighted and what was once a battle of wills became a time of pleasure. Sandra had a similar reluctance to rise and shine but when her parents offered a half hour of television before breakfast, the problem was removed.

At three and a half, children are emotionally fragile and very fearful, fearful of noises, unexpected events, anything "broken." They may be fearful at the playground and refuse to go down the slide or climb the jungle gym. A parent who doesn't understand the issues of this age might force the child to do the tasks with the idea that you have to face your "fears," become a man. The child would probably protest. The parent would insist. There would be a battle royal. The child might then experience himself as "bad" and shameful for distressing his parents or weak and powerless for not winning the battle or both. All of these outcomes would result in a low self-esteem for the child with numerous negative outcomes in adulthood.

The knowledgeable parent would empathize with the child's fears; would support and help him by holding his hand; going with him down the slide; examining the noises and explaining their "naturalness." The child and adult can write a book about the fears and how children might cope with them. If one activity produces too much anxiety, a parent might simply suggest another activity. The knowledgeable parent can accumulate much good information from books, techniques to use that are helpful. The knowledgeable parent also knows that children are different and will study his own child to understand their particular needs and devise creative means to address them. The consequences of this route is that the child will feel heard, understood, "normal" and supported and helped. He will learn that he doesn't have to be perfect to be loved and, that if he needs help, he can trust that people will help him. So, this knowledgeable activity will not only result in more peaceful, happy times in the present but will help produce a child with high self-esteem who has faith in himself and in the people who love him.

At five years old, Timothy was a parental dream. He loved himself; he loved his parents. He was invested in being good, in pleasing, in doing things right. He felt positive about the world and delighted by his environment.
He wanted very much to be mature and to do grownup things.
He loved to talk, to learn new things, to read, to experiment with writing

his own name and simple words. Now Timothy is five and a half.

Suddenly, he is both passive and explosive. He can be extremely withdrawn one minute and obnoxiously bold the next.

He can be sweet one minute and mean the next. He sulks; he bursts into tears; he has tantrums, colds, headaches, ear aches. Dora and Steve were educated parents. They had read the books, participated in a parenting group and had an aunt who was a child therapist. They knew enough to enjoy and cherish the sunniness of their five-year-old; to be prepared for the disequilibrium at five-and-a-half and to have strategies and tools to navigate the difficulties.

And so it goes. Children change from day to day and from year to year. They have places to go and tasks to accomplish. For example, a willful two year old is not battling to cause trouble. He is battling to achieve autonomy - a measure of being powerful in the world. An engaged adolescent who screams at his parents that he hates them is not trying to cause pain - nor does he, in fact, hate them. His task is separation - the need to move away from, be independent of his parents; to begin the process of becoming an adult and anger is a way to accomplish distance and individuation.

And so it goes. The child moves from age to age and stage to stage on his journey to adulthood. The parents also move from age to age and stage to stage, becoming different parents through the journey. A one-year-old needs a parent who is always there, always available, who can "read" his signals and respond quickly to his needs, who is physically and verbally affectionate. There is no real place for discipline and limits because a one-year-old understands very little of that. On the other hand, an adolescent needs lots of space from the parents -- lots of room to discover himself

17.

and clear and appropriate discipline and limits. An adolescent also needs affection and nurturing but in a wholly different measure and form than a one-year-old.

Parents who have educated themselves in ages and stages, appropriate discipline, strategies and coping techniques, tensional outlets, physical and emotional and intellectual milestones, healthy forms of interactions with their children at different crossroads, parents who have support people to aid them and counsel them, come to the task of parenting aware and prepared. They understand what they see and what to do about it. The work is still very hard but the outcome is very likely to be productive for them, for their child and for the community at large. Parents who come to their task with nothing but goodwill will find the task daunting, frustrating, impossible, overwhelming, unpleasant and will probably raise unhappy damaged children. On the silliest and most basic level, imagine a serious leak in your home. Would you prefer a competent, experienced plumber or your next door neighbor who has never done it before and he has no real idea of what he's doing. Unfortunately, most of our children have to endure the nextdoor neighbor.

The second part of being a knowledgeable, competent parent is to know yourself and to learn to manage yourself in a healthy way. Most of us do not know ourselves. We know aspects of ourselves while we choose to ignore or deny other aspects or pieces of ourselves. Blanche will tell everyone that she is the most generous person in the world, and, to some extent that is true. If you are in trouble, Blanche will appear. She will listen to your woes. She will offer sympathy or money or a home-cooked meal or to accompany you to the doctor…What Blanche doesn't know is that when her friends are not in "trouble," she disappears.
The phone calls can stop for months at a time.

There will be no offers of companionship; happy events will not be celebrated; good news will not be applauded or exchanged. Blanche's friends feel confused, frustrated and abandoned and deeply hurt but Blanche can not hear or understand that. Richard thinks of himself as a charming, warm, sociable, entertaining man who has a thousand friends. And, that is true. In social situations, Richard is funny and articulate and engaging. He speaks well; has endless stories to recount and multiple ways to connect. At home, in his living room, Richard drinks and, then, he sits morose and glowering on the couch, half-watching the sports events and half nodding sleepily. His children are afraid of his black moods and tiptoe around him. His wife occupies herself in the kitchen as they all hope he won't explode. Richard does not own that piece of himself. He has buried that knowledge in a trunk at the back of his psyche and knows himself only as a "good fellow." Rita knows that she has a hair trigger where her anger is concerned. She is irritated by everything. Any negative occurrence elicits screaming, crying, plate throwing but Rita thinks that this is "normal." This is what she knows; this is what she saw her Mother do for thirty years of her life. Rita has a daughter who is seven. She is very shy and scared, frightened of going to school, frightened of noises, failing her classes, having nightmares often. Rita does not connect her daughter's situation and emotional demeanor with the constant rage that she has to endure.

Sarah and Paul are very anxious people. They worry constantly about everything -- money, terrorist attacks, sudden illness in the family, cancer, losing their jobs, the refrigerator breaking down...Their conversations are constant litanies of the horrible things that are happening or the horrible things that might happen. An umbrella of dread hangs on the house. Cecil, their older son, 12, is never home. When he isn't at school, he's playing baseball or hockey or riding his bike or hiding out in friends' houses. He's running from the black cloud that is his home. Mickey, who is 9, is not so fortunate. He cannot run. He's frightened of leaving the house and needs to be dragged, kicking and crying to school. He is unable to concentrate on school work and mainly fails his classes. He has no friends; he doesn't play. He ruminates in his head scenarios of disaster.

Trisha has a thirty-five-year-old daughter who is married and has two children. Whether in conversation on the telephone or in person, Trisha constantly monitors her daughter's activities and constantly scolds her for what she is doing "wrong," where she's failing and what the "right" way is. There is only one "right" way and Trisha is the holder of that treasure. Trisha has noticed that her daughter calls her very rarely. She has noticed that the invitations to visit are few. She has noticed the brisk, aggravated tone in her daughter's voice and the fact that she rarely sees her grandchildren. She feels sad and hurt and lonely and confused but she has not connected these results with her behavior.

Let me take a moment here to say that being a good parent does not stop when your children leave home as adults. Knowing how to be a good parent to adult children is a special art and requires as much thought and care and knowledge as being a parent to small children. There are too many families living in anger and hurt and disappointment because the parents cannot be appropriate, cannot give the adult children the freedom and respect they need to make authentic choices, cannot help and support approximately, cannot give the approval and positive feedback that people crave.

Christopher was a photographer, just beginning his career. He was very talented

and having a good beginning but struggling as all twenty-five-year- olds do.
He needed to buy some very important equipment and had secured a loan from the
bank and asked his financially stable Mother to co-sign the loan. She refused.
Christopher had to go to a friend for help. He subsequently became a
very successful photographer as he had been a very successful student…
He never understood his Mother's action, never forgave her and lived with
the pain and disappointment his whole life.

Penny fell in love with a wonderful man. He was intelligent and kind and educated
and treated her wonderfully well. He and Penny had many things in common.
They were both teachers; they were both politically active; they both sang in choirs
--- However, Penny's boyfriend, Tim, was not Jewish. Penny's parents who
were not Orthodox or even particularly religious, hounded her to give him up,
and when she wouldn't, they declared her "dead" to them. Penny hasn't seen her
parents in twenty years.

Gerald lost his job. For ten years, he had been a successful architect, working
for a firm that required him to work twelve hours a day. Tense and exhausted,
he finally confronted his boss on his need for a better work schedule. When his
boss flatly refused, Gerald lost his temper and was immediately fired. Several
weeks later, Gerald tried to tell his Mother how sad and disappointed he was
feeling and how nervous about the future. His Mother's comment was,
"That will teach you to give up a well paying job." Shocked and disgusted, Gerald
hung up the phone, feeling very alone, misunderstood and uncared about.
Many memories surfaced where his Mother had not been there for him or had
made him feel "wrong" about any misfortune that came his way.

Many of us have angry, inpatient, critical, killing, wiping out, explosive, terrified pieces in our personalities. Often, we are unaware of these pieces and they leak out everywhere, unchecked, even, and especially in our parenting. Some of us are aware of these pieces but we don't know how to manage them so they still continue to leak out everywhere, especially with our children.

To become better parents and better people, we need to become aware and conscious of all of our pieces -- what they are, where they are, how they manifest and where they are destructive and, then, we need to find means and strategies to control them rather than they controlling us.

The best way is to find a good therapist and to settle into a long term process. In good therapy, the person will have an opportunity to examine their past, their history, to uncover the repetitive patterns that drive them and to change those patterns that are destructive to themselves and others. Change is not easy. We are hard wired, programmed in certain patterns. We are compelled to repeat them over and over, no matter how painful and hurtful they are to ourselves and others. Because they are what we've always known, we feel comfortable with them and don't want to give them up. To change them means moving out of our comfort zone, struggling, failing, struggling again…That takes bravery and discipline and very hard work but the results are worth it.

Mona came from a home where everything and everyone was expected to be perfect. The house was always spotless; the children's appearance was scrutinized minutely before they left the house. Everything less than an A was not an acceptable grade; holidays were celebrated with great pomp and circumstance;

manners had to be impeccable; others were constantly berated for their shortcomings. Mona's Father drank heavily; her Mother was always exhausted and on numerous psychotropic medications and there was an umbrella of gloom and anxiety in the house, everyone waiting for the bomb to blow but Mona was a child and never connected the atmosphere in the house with her parents' perfectionism.

One day, Mona was on the playground with her three-year-old son and she found herself yelling at him with great vehemence that he was coming down the slide too slowly. First she saw the look of confusion on her son's face. Then, she heard his sobs. And, Mona had a moment of clarity. She realized how silly she was being, how damaging; she remembered her Mother yelling at her that she wasn't using the Play-Doh "correctly" and Mona took herself to therapy. Three years later, she was a much happier woman with a much happier child.

Olga and Hank were big achievers. They both had PHD's; they both had high positions in their chosen field; they both worked endless hours but they both earned high salaries. They were proud of their achievements and thought of themselves as very special.

Naturally they sent their son Peter to a highly academic school that emphasized scholarly achievement. There were endless parental meetings to discuss grade point averages, ways to improve scores and special high schools to apply to. They themselves had endless talks with Peter about how important it was that he should achieve.

Slowly, they began to notice that Peter was becoming reluctant to go to school;

was hiding his report cards; seemed shy and withdrawn and had no friends. Worried, they set up a meeting with the school counselor who was also a therapist. In the subsequent sessions, they began to see that they were repeating their parental patterns. Only achievement was valued in their homes. They remembered how sad and lonely and unloved they often felt; they remembered the stomach aches before tests; they remembered the dancing lessons and art classes and roller skating they were not allowed to do because only grades were important; they remembered the disappointment on their parents' faces when they did not become valedictorians; they remembered the arguments about their marriage because Hank wasn't making enough money. They realized quickly that they were doing to Peter what had been done to them.

They took Peter out of the "prestigious" school and found him a more "normal" school where the one and only emphasis was not on grades. They found interests that Peter wanted to pursue like the drama club and the karate class. They began to encourage friends and sleepovers. They made sure that any positive achievements were acknowledged and applauded and that problems were addressed, but, with love and support rather than humiliation and condemnation. These changes were not easy to make, but, they worked to make them and, eventually, had a much happier child in a much happier home.

Nina was bewildered by her attitude to her ten-year-old daughter. Of course, she loved her. She was proud of her. She admired her beauty, her intelligence, her sense of humor but she was also jealous of her husband's attention to her; wanted to feel "better" than her, wanted to deprive her of "goodies," wanted to take away her friends. Bewildered and conflicted,

Nina took herself to therapy and discovered that she was transferring onto her daughter the difficult and contentious relationship that she had had with her twin sister. Realizing that, in reality, the two relationships had nothing in common and were totally unconnected, Nina was able to become a more loving and appropriate Mother.

For people for whom therapy is not an option because of money or inclination or time or fear, there are parenting support groups where parents meet and look at themselves, their parenting choices and their histories. Sharing with others often triggers consciousness, wisdom, awareness of problems and thought through solutions. Often an expert may lead the group and help point out what parents aren't seeing or parents can do for each other. In the 60's the head start program had as one of it's main features parenting groups where parents met to discuss their experiences, parenting skills, problems, aspirations, techniques. As a leader of these groups, I saw first hand how helpful they could be to parents and how glorious they could be for the children who benefited from everything the parents learned. We need to establish parenting groups in our schools, in our hospitals, in our communities as a regular feature of our lives to underline how critical good parenting is, how absent it often is and that attention must be paid, work must be done, time must be spent for the welfare of our children.

Another possibility for parents is to find themselves a mentor, a parent in the family or in the social circle or community who has raised good adults -- loving people who love themselves and others, who find joy in living, who are active in creating good lives. Access this mentor, ask them for help, advice, guidance -- explore your dilemmas with them -- explore your personal struggles -- be honest about your "pieces." Great and good help could be forthcoming.

Parenting involves numerous aspects of concern that need attention and focus. Firstly there is the physical health of the child -- the need to be disciplined about doctor's appointments and vaccinations and dental health and optometric issues and nutrition and allergies and special conditions. Then, there is the need to provide mental stimulation for the child. Books have to be read to awaken an interest in creativity and learning. Music has to be played and enjoyed to awaken the senses. Games have to be played to introduce logic and thinking and attention span and problem solving. Practical matters have to occur to help the child cope better and feel powerful learning letters and numbers, how to count and, later, science projects and arts and crafts and trips to broaden the thinking and become aware of other cultures. Children have to be talked to about life and the world, their concerns. Questions have to be answered deeply and respectfully.

Social skills have to be addressed. Not only do children have to be taught manners and empathy and cooperation and caring and sharing, they have to be given numerous opportunities to interact with others, both in groups and one on one so they can learn to be social and intimate and truly human. That involves regular play dates and interest groups and camps and birthday celebrations and, later, sleepovers and pajama parties and mixed gender parties, etc.

And, then, there are numerous other areas of great importance -- discipline which changes as your child changes -- homework, sibling rivalry, sex education, sexual orientation, acting-out behavior, the uses of and dangers of technology -----

In the 70's, a very wise man, Haim Ginott wrote several books on how to speak to your child. He enumerated the many ways that unconscious parents spoke in humiliating down-putting terms to their children; the noxious effect that this kind of communication has on a child's self-esteem and on the parent-child relationship. He spoke about how parents gave verbal solutions to a child's problems instead of helping the child problem solve himself and find answers for himself. He gave numerous examples of how parents don't hear and don't listen and suggested techniques of connection that would strengthen the family bond and enrich the child's sense of self. The point of this reference is that there are vast areas of necessary knowledge that one has to access in order to do a good parenting job.

Here is one brief story of a child who did not have the advantage of good parenting and how it affected not only him but society at large.

Kenneth was an only child raised by two abusive parents. His father, an accountant, drank regularly and, when he was not nodding off on the sofa, he was throwing up all over the house. He totally ignored Kenneth for endless hours and endless days until, for no apparent reason, he would explode, scream, hit and throw things. His Mother was a meek housewife, terrified of her husband, terrified of her child, and terrified of everyone and everything. She spent most of her time in bed and used Kenneth as her parent, expecting him to clean and cook and remember her medications and rub her feet and listen to her woes about her marriage. Kenneth grew up painfully lonely, miserably terrified and enraged. When he was seven he was beating up and humiliating younger children on a regular schedule. He was expelled from school numerous times but the school authorities had neither the will nor the knowledge to intervene appropriately so Kenneth continued. As he grew older, he grew bolder, and, at twelve, accused two teachers and a priest of molesting him. By the time those individuals extracted themselves from the charge, their lives were in tatters and Kenneth was in a juvenile facility. He came out at fifteen, moved in with a prostitute, impregnated her and conceived two children, both of whom died of abuse and neglect. Again, the system was remiss. They did not pursue diligently, did not investigate properly and Kenneth was released on a technicality. At twenty-three, a drunk like his Father, with a drug-addicted wife, he tried to rob a liquor store. He shot the proprietor and three innocent customers before he was finally apprehended, sent to prison, and, for a while, society at large was saved from blatant damage but not from the damage of paying for his prison and not from the damage that he propagated in prison. Thus the domino effect and the domino misery of bad parenting.

Of course, Kenneth is an extreme example of what can and does go wrong but there are also more subtle effects of bad parenting that spoil people's lives and spoil the lives or, at least, negatively affect the lives of those they live with, work with, come in contact with intimately or peripherally.

Shelby was the head of marketing at a prestigious department store. Raised by a very controlling, down-putting Mother, he repeated this behavior with his employees. Not only did he insist that they work unspeakable hours but he demanded a perfection that could not exist, and, when that elusive perfection didn't occur, he would erupt in a tirade of name calling and humiliation of anyone in his path. His employees became depressed, developed headaches, gained pounds, lost pounds, walked around enraged and powerless and miserable, terrified in a bad economy and powerless because Shelby was the nephew of the CEO and untouchable.

Thus misery causes misery and mushrooms.

All of us have been in situations where we were caused pain and abuse by people who themselves were pained and abused.

Mary was raised in a very religious household. There were endless rules to follow, endless "good deeds" to accomplish, sacrifices to be made and "sins" to be avoided. Every minute aspect of her day and life were examined and judged. All negative feelings were rejected as "bad;" all wants were determined to be "selfish." Self-sacrifice was the highest good. Mary grew up terrified. She controlled the terror by obsessive "good" behavior unaware of how enraged she was underneath all the "goodness." Mary became a nun, a teacher and a Mother Superior. Throughout her life, she was unaware of the extent and quality of her rage. She lived by humiliating, shaming, wiping out, hitting her students, the nuns in her care and everyone who had the bad fortune to be in her world.

Senator Archibald Brown was fathered by a criminal, a man who indulged in endless schemes to defraud others. A sociopath, smart and endlessly charming, he defrauded people of their money, their reputations, their well-being. He held his son close, taught him everything he knew and paid his way into the Senate. The Senator's constituents don't know that they have a criminal in their midst who will use them and abuse them in any way he sees fit to meet his own ends.

The effects of bad parenting are everywhere -- and, especially visible in the lives of our celebrities. In the 1920's Dorothy Parker was considered one of the wittiest women in America.

An international poet and short story writer and Hollywood screen writer, she knew everyone -- Lillian Hellman, William Faulkner, the Fitzeralds, Sara and Gerald Murphy... An honored member of the Algonquin Round Table, she was invited everywhere. To the naked eye, she seemed to have everything worth having and to know everyone worth knowing.

Yet, behind the glamorous, "successful" life was a woman who drank heavily all her life, who made a string of suicide attempts, had abortions, who was often in despairing debt, who had two broken marriages and a series of abusive love affairs and whose general sadness and rage is very evident in her work.

Oh, I should like to ride the seas,
A roaring buccaneer,
A cutglass banging at my knees,
A dirk behind my ear.
And when my captives' chains would clank
I'd howl with glee and drink,
And then fling out the quivering plank
And watch the beggars sink.

Dorothy was the last of four children. Her Mother was forty-two when she was born, approaching menopause and unhappy with the new arrival. Dorothy was raised by servants who came and went. Mother died when Dorothy was five and Dorothy blamed herself for her Mother's death. We see here a history of maternal abandonment, first emotional, then, physical. When that happens, usually the result is abandonment depression -- a great sense of loneliness, sadness, anger, emptiness and anger against the self since all children believe that they cause the negative things that happen in their lives. The emptiness generally translates to addictions and here we see the alcohol abuse and, also, often the lavish spending. Her anger toward her Mother is evident in her writing. Her short stories are empty of any loving Mothers. Most of the Mothers are indifferent or actively abusive to their children.

In "Little Curtis," for example the Mother adopts a little four-year-old boy and, then, treats him sadistically. Dorothy's anger against the self is evident in consistently self-destructive behavior. In school, she was the trouble maker. Brilliant, she, nevertheless, left school at fourteen. Her first marriage was to an alcoholic, addicted to morphine who tried to gas himself. Subsequently, she had a long string of relationships with abusive men who hurt her, cheated on her or used her. In her working life, she was often late or absent to hand in work, causing herself great difficulty with editors and publishers. She alienated friends and people who had helped her or wanted to help her until she ended up alone, in squalid, penniless circumstances, ill and morbidly depressed.

It is important to say that aside from her maternal traumas, Dorothy also suffered other family issues and difficulties. Her father very quickly married a stepmother whom Dorothy despised. When that stepmother, suddenly, died, Dorothy once more blamed herself. She experienced her father as selfish and tyrannical and her siblings as "noisy and jokey" and alien. She felt disconnected from all of her family, so much so, that none of them were invited to her wedding or played any meaningful part in her life. She wiped them out as she felt wiped out by them.

What she did not realize, as most of us don't is that while she was spewing rage, outwardly, everywhere, she was turning this rage inwardly, on herself and punishing herself with the choices she made in her living.

Vincent Van Gogh is a legendary artist whose fame is worldwide and whose work is worshipped by multitudes for it's beauty, power and soul. Yet, Vincent Van Gogh is also the man who spent time in a lunatic asylum, who took a cudgel to bed with him and belabored his back with it, who slept outside in winter without bed or blankets, who lost every job and every relationship he ever had, who mutilated his ear, and ultimately shot himself dead at the age of thirty-seven.

What was responsible for this masochism, this self-hatred, this so negative outcome in a man so intelligent and so hugely talented?

Vincent was one of six children. It is a rare parent who has enough energy and time and resources to pay very close attention to and really nurture six children. Vincent was labeled the "unruly one" in his family as opposed to Theo who was the "good" one so he was early made to feel inferior and not "right." His Mother said of him that "wherever Vincent may be or whatever he may do, he will spoil everything." Thus we see Vincent's life as a prophecy fulfilled. Vincent stated in his letters that he felt unloved and deprived and recalled his youth as very unhappy. When he saw the real love that existed between his lover Ursula and her Mother, he was astonished and announced that he never knew such love existed.

An unloved, criticized child blames himself for the situation and punishes himself for his "badness."

Aside from a cold and critical Mother, Vincent had to endure very strict discipline. There were rigid rules in the household and, when young, the children were not permitted to leave the parsonage garden or play with other children.

Vincent's Father was a Dutch reformed minister steeped in Calvinism. Calvinism favored making money. Making money became a religious act. Poverty was seen as shameful. How shameful must Vincent have felt in a family peopled into high ranking clergy, generals and admirals when he had no money and had to be supported by his brother!

Vincent experienced his Father as obstinate, unintelligent, cold and narrow minded. He experienced his youth as gloomy, cold and sterile. He was so disappointed with his family that he never used Van Gogh as a signature on any of his paintings -- only Vincent. "I find Father's and Mother's sermons and ideas about God, people, morality and virtue a lot of stuff and nonsense."

However, as enraged as Vincent was at his family, there was a greater rage that was turned against himself, because, somewhere, like all children, he accepted the messages that he was bad and unworthy and rejected. He was sent to boarding school when he was eleven, and accepting those messages, he, unconsciously set out to punish himself for his "badness" and punish himself he did.

Michael Jackson was the seventh of nine children. Both his parents worked. It is hard to imagine that he could, in these circumstances, possibly get the close individual attention and nurturing that a child needs to feel good about himself, lovable, important, special -- all the elements that lead to a healthy self-esteem. Children who are not given time and attention and respect for what they feel and need, often grow up with a feeling of vast emptiness that they then try to fill with food or alcohol or drugs or sex. In his autobiography, Michael says that he was never close to his Father, that his Father had a "shell around him." When a Father distances himself, children often blame themselves, feel worthless and unlovable and unconsciously, punish themselves in a myriad of ways as Michael did. Sometimes, what these children do is they strive to be "perfect" -- to please the unpleasable parent and, finally, be loved. Michael did that. As a child, he worked at a nightclub five, six nights a week. Even when he was sick, he was expected to work. In his book, he identifies his perfectionism and how, throughout his life, he has strived to please everyone all the time.

He talks about his Father's rage, how he was hit all the time, and, how when he protested, he was hit even more. When children are beaten, they feel wrong and bad and powerless and, again, find unconscious ways to punish themselves as Michael did with drugs. His many surgeries and attempts to make himself look different speak volumes to his dissatisfaction with himself --
a dissatisfaction engendered by a rejecting, distant Father and a demand to constantly and always powerlessly obey.

Statements in his book: "I'm one of the loneliest people in the world."
"I'm poor in moments of true joy." "I had very few friends and felt very isolated."

The saddest statements in <u>Moonwalk</u> concern his interest in "the way Elvis
destroyed himself." "I don't ever want to walk those grounds myself." He also
considers the "tragedy" of Marilyn Monroe and Jimi Hendrix and how they
"cheated" their fans because they died of drugs and liquor.

How sad that this talented and wonderful little boy was himself cheated by his
history and upbringing into a difficult, painful life and an unfortunate
early and untimely death.

Adolf Hitler is a prime example of a damaged child who brings grief and
destruction, not only to himself, but to others, in this case 50 million people.

Hitler's father, Alois, was illegitimate. There is a good possibility that Hitler's
grandfather was a wealthy Jew and that Hitler's grandmother was a domestic in the
household and the young son had gotten the grandmother, Marie Anna, pregnant.
It is possible that there is where the unconscious hostility to Jews began.
His Father had a very hard time. His Mother died early and his stepfather abandoned
him. He ran away from home when he was thirteen, went to Vienna and
became first a shoemaker, and, then, later a civil servant and customs inspector.

It is a truism in psychology that people who are abandoned, neglected and badly
parented often repeat that with their own children. Alois Sr. was reported to be harsh

with his children, a strict disciplinarian, exacting and pedantic who showed no affection to Adolf and, indeed, thrashed him with a whip every day of his life. He was a drunk who demanded absolute obedience and when he didn't get it, would hit, humiliate. Once he held Adolf to the back of a tree till he lost consciousness. Alois Jr. was treated equally badly. When children are treated with such cruelty, they become enraged. Terrified to turn the anger against the perpetrator, they turn it against themselves or displace it on others. In Alois Jr.'s case, he resented Adolf for receiving preferential treatment from his stepmother and Adolf became a butt of his anger so the young boy Adolf was served every day a platter of rage, abuse and neglect. There must have built in him a caldron of rage and hostility which he, later found a way to express and displace.

A key element in the successful raising of healthy children is a stable, structured, ordered environment. In a structured environment, life is predictable. Children know what will happen. They can count on events repeating themselves in an orderly manner. When events are predictable, one feels more in control, safer. Adolf Hitler's life was the opposite of that.

Adolf's father was a womanizer with many mistresses. He brought a sixteen-year-old into the household and had an affair with her. His wife left him. The maid gave birth to a son, illegitimate. After his first wife died, he married Fannie and they had a daughter. Fannie, however had a series of lung ailments and was forced to move to the country, leaving the father with the two infants. He brought in the niece Klara and she became the mistress and then the nursemaid. When Fannie died, Klara married her uncle and had three children so there were five children in the household.

Then the three children died and she had Adolf. When Adolf was five, his brother was born. Father was assigned to another city and the family stayed behind so Adolf experienced a parental abandonment which can cause depression in children. When his family reunited, there were five children, including a crying infant. His Father continued to drink heavily and rage constantly. There was nothing in this upbringing to suggest that the world was anything but a chaotic, unsafe mess where people were not to be trusted. Thus, enraged and boiling from years of horrific abuse and neglect, powerless from constant disrespect, Adolf found a way to gain "power" and detonate the bomb inside him.

Sometimes, we hear the words directly from the abused children. We hear the stories and the outcome of their stories.

From Jeanette Winterson in <u>Why Be Happy When You Could Be Normal?</u>
"When my Mother was angry with me, which was often, she said,
'The devil has led us to the wrong crib.' "
"I was beaten as a child and I learned early never to cry.
If I was locked out overnight, I sat on the doorstep till the milkman came.
"Until I was two years old, I screamed. Child psychology hadn't reached Accrington and in spite of important work by Winnicott, Bowlby and Balint on attachment and the trauma of early separation from the love object that is the Mother, a screaming baby wasn't a hurt baby, it was a devil baby."
"I was often full of rage and despair. I was always lonely." "I was damaged and a very important part of me had been destroyed."
"In school I was given bad reports in the way that bad children are given bad reports.

I had accepted the label. It was better to have some identity than none at all."

"I had no understanding of family life. I had no understanding that you could like your parents or that they could love you enough to let you be yourself."
"I was thinking of suicide because it had to be an option. Language left me. I was in the place before I had any language. The abandoned place."
"I was locked in the coal bin often."
"I was beaten by my Father regularly, every time he was instructed by my Mother."
"In February, I tried to end my life."

Those words come from Ms. Winterson's heart and soul, a crying testament to the suffering and pain she endured and to the repercussions of such an upbringing.

Every day, every moment, her story and her anguish are being repeated and revisited in homes -- rich and poor -- all over America and all over the world

In Life Is Not A Stage, Florence Henderson speaks movingly and painfully about the traumas of her childhood and what they have wrought. "As a young child I endured abuse and abandonment because of alcoholism. We suffer a guilt syndrome in one form or another because we are powerless to help at the time. If we're not paralyzed by fear, anger, hatred or numbed by our own addictions, we have to overcome deep-seated reactive patterns… We grow up to become control freaks to keep the real or imagined chaos away. Others become gregarious caregivers trying to please everybody except ourselves. And many, including yours truly, end up with most of the above."

She was born to a very poor farmer who was an alcoholic, an exploder and sexually abusive. Her mother could not handle the situation and left the family when Florence was twelve. Love, nurturing and kindness were virtually non- existant so though the lonely, abandoned, terrified child went on to a sparkling career, she also went on to bouts of soul beating depression, blaming herself for everything that didn't work, guilt at being depressed, terrror of performing, terror of flying, alcoholism, adultery, inability to confront, inability to solve problems -----

Thus, no matter how high the glory, damaged children lead damaged lives. Knowledgeable, educated parenting is the antidote to damage.

A Mother took her three children to Central Park. They played hide and seek, climbed some rocks, floated boats on the water and had lunch. Then the Mother gathered the children and asked them to play at the bottom of the hill while she climbed to the top and stayed there. They called for her attention, they sang her questions. She was quiet and unresponsive. Finally one child screemed with frustration, "What are you doing up there?" And her voice answered sweetly, "I'm making you a good Mother."

There is a wise lesson in that. Parents who want to take good and careful care of their children need also to take good and careful care of themselves. It is hard, exhausting, backbreaking work to be a good parent and without "feeding" oneself, one can't "feed" the other.

What does that, specifically, mean. It means taking care of your physical health --

going to doctors regularly, eating healthy, finding time to exercise regularly.
It means putting aside time to "date" your husband -- to have fun time together
and sexual time together. It means finding time to nuture and enjoy your friendships.
It means finding time for your "passions" if you have them. It means finding a
small space everyday to just breathe and be.

I can hear mothers muttering to themselves that I'm either crazy, have never had
children or am wealthy and have endless help at my command. I know how hard it
is but if people are organized and creative, much is possible. For example -- if your
baby is small and in a carriage, you can get a running carriage where you are with
your baby while doing your exercise. Instead of sitting on a bench and watching
your children play, participate. Run up and down the stairs, come down the slide,
hang on the bars, play a running game of hide and go seek. When you're teaching
your kids to swim, ferry them across the pool. Make a game out of it and they will
love it and you will be getting your exercise.

Form a Mother co-op where the children can play and socialize while the Mothers
exchange confidences, information or laughter or where some Mothers stay while
others pursue their own plans. Join a "Y" group or neighborhood Mommy & Me
group that serves the same purpose.

The "Y" in my neighborhood has a group where Moms do yoga while babies watch
at times and participate at others. When children get older, they can have their own
activities e.g. karate groups, music groups, art classes where parents can
have a few hours to and for themselves.

Invite your family and acquaintances in. Not only can grandparents babysit and entertain but a favorite aunt, the next door neighbor, the teacher at the local nursery. A friend of mine had a neighbor whose four-year-old grandson lived in England. She missed him very much and was only too happy to visit with and play with my friend's four-year-old son. Another acquaintance had a cleaning person who came only once a week but she became so fond of he children that she volunteered without pay, to spend time with them and even to take them to events for which she paid.

Open your eyes, open your mind, think creatively. There are endless possibilities.

Sometimes we have to postpone our passions. There is only so much time in the day, only so much energy that one person has. Perhaps you wanted to be a painter, or a writer or a lawyer and there is no time for that now and you have to postpone. You need to know that children grow, that they go to school; they become more independent and, somewhere, down the line, your dreams will wait for you. Meanwhile, you can plan and you can participate on a small scale. Take the once a week acting class; take your children "painting" while you really paint, offer to volunteer several hours at a law firm or nursery school or hospital so you become acquainted with your future environment and breathe in the air.

Don't forget yourself. To generously give to others, you have to also feed yourself. With careful thought and careful planning, you will find the ways to do it.

The foundation of any family is the relationship of the couple so whilst this relationship is terrifically important to you, it's also important, nay, critical to your children. A stable, communicative, affectionate, loving relationship between the parents fosters a sense of safety for the children, trust in relationships, trust in people -- the idea that they are safe in the world and can relax in that safety. So parents have to find the time to have fun with each other, time to have sex with each other, time to solve practical issues. My recommendation to couples is to set a date night or date times and to keep those religiously -- honoring them and nurturing them and creating good times with and for each other. Date times are times to enjoy -- they are never times to argue about issues or responsibilities or perceived failures. Those situations, common in every family are relegated to business meetings -- a time, every week, where couples sit down and explore problems, practical, emotional, situational and attempt to solve them and move forward.

Just as we are not taught to parent so are we not taught to be in a relationship. The result is that, no matter how much you love your partner, you may not have the tools to manage a successful relationship. If you come from a home where there was only one "right" way to do everything, you will be in constant combat about the "right" way. If you were wiped out and devalued as a child, you will either allow yourself to be devalued and discounted and feel enraged about it or you will devalue and discount your partner. If it was unsafe in your home of origin to trust and communicate, then you will not trust and not communicate, and, then, you will not really be married because a good marriage is based on trust and communication. If you were a spoiled child, then, you will, probably, be a spoiled adult and will either never feel like you're getting enough or will give nothing and grab as much as you can.

When you see these issues intruding on the love and hope, consider a marriage helpful in identifying the issues and moving forward in a positive fashion.

I can hear the comments. "What's the matter with her? Where are we
Supposed to find the time? Where are we supposed to find the money?"
I understand the difficulties but if you had diabetes or migraine headaches or
acid reflux, you would find the time to go to a doctor. This is equally critical,
equally important and needs to be addressed. The outcome will be growth,
happiness, satisfaction, a healthier family and a model for the children on
how to work for happiness, health and productivity.

It came to me that it would be interesting to do a very informal survey of people's
thoughts about the issue of parenting so I approached a variety of men and women,
young and old, straight and gay, parents and non-parents with the question --

"What do you think is the most important thing to know about parenting?

" What follows are the multiple, myriad, varied responses.

1) That children need to be discovered, not molded.

2) Take the time to be patient, to be present; let them explore and show you things.

3) Unconditional love.

4) Patience and honesty.

5) Communication and love.

6) Unconditional love. Positive modeling behavior.

7) Loving your children.

8) There is not one right way to parent. It depends on you, your child, time and circumstances.

9) Accepting your children for who they are.

10) Understanding.

11) To keep the lines of communication open.

12) Striking a balance between discipline and encouragement. Never strike a child -- ever.

13) Rather than concentrate on making money, concentrating on giving the children the time and attention they need.

14) Selfless patience.

15) They should know that parenting is very hard work. They should remember what it's like to be a child.

16) Discipline. Parents and children need to have control of their feelings and learn to discipline themselves.

17) Creating a sense of safety for the child. Communicating, explaining things.

18) Give your child self-esteem, self-worth. Help them value themselves.

19) Accepting the child for who they are.

20) Listen. Use your "no's sparingly. Think before you speak.

In reviewing the responses, many thoughts occurred to me. I was gratified by the thoughtfulness of people and the wisdom of the responses. On the other hand, it was fascinating to me that none of these people mentioned the importance of knowledgeable, educated parenting. How do you give your child a sense of self-worth? How do you learn to listen? Where does one learn to not say "no" too much?

How do you establish the appropriate priorities so your children get the attention they need? How do you learn to accept your child as they are rather than mold them into who you need them to be? In order to know and understand and be able to do, we have to first learn, -- learn about what children need, learn about ourselves -- our own character and prejudices and blind spots. Only when we take the time and patience to learn and know can we have the tools to be good, effective parents.

This is my desperate, heartfelt plea for people to hear, to listen, to think about the importance of good parenting, to institute that in their own lives and to disseminate it to their friends, their neighbors and society as a whole.
It is my desperate hope that society will open an ongoing dialogue about the critical importance of knowledgeable parenting so that there are TV shows that discuss, regularly, parenting issues, that there are many institutions e.g. schools, colleges, libraries that offer parenting courses, that school personnel realize the vital importance to their students of their home life and atmosphere and consider and attend to that aspect of a child's life, that knowledgeable experts blog about parenting and offer themselves as speakers to parenting groups or community meetings, that knowledgeable, educated parenting become a national priority so that we can raise happy, healthy children and, ultimately, kind, knowledgeable, caring citizens.

ACKNOWLEDGEMENTS

To my amazing patients who have taught me everything I know about good and bad parenting, thank you.

To my family and friends who have been interested in, supportive of and helpful with my project, thank you.

To my assistant, Gilda Konrad, whose practical help was immeasurable, thank you.

To Theodora Borsen, whose art and skill are considerable and who helped with the art and design of this book, thank you.

To Richard Phibbs, photographer extraordinaire whose talent made me look good, thank you.

To all parents who try every day, thank you.

To my amazing and powerful daughters, Avra and Paulette, thank you for being.

May good parenting rule the world!

www.ingramcontent.com/pod-product-compliance
Lightning Source LLC
Chambersburg PA
CBHW071745020426
42331CB00008B/2191